DIGITAL MINDS

THE PSYCHOLOGICAL EVOLUTION IN ENHANCED TECHNOLOGY AND SOCIAL SITES

Table of Contents

1. Introduction: The Digital Revolution

2. The Rise of Social Media: A Historical Overview

3. The Psychological Impact of Social Networking

4. The Role of Algorithms: Shaping Our Thoughts

5. Cyberpsychology: Understanding Online Behaviour

6. The Impact of Technology on Mental Health

7. Digital Identity: Crafting Personas Online

8. Influence of Social Media on Self-Esteem & Body Image

9. The Social Comparison Theory in the Digital Age

10. Online Relationships: Friendship, Romance & Community

11. Digital Detox: The Need for a Break from Technology

12. The Role of Technology in Education and Learning

13. The Future of Work: Remote Working and Digital Collaboration

14. Privacy and Security in the Age of Social Media

15. Conclusion: Navigating the Digital World

INTRODUCTION: THE DIGITAL REVOLUTION

The advent of the internet and the proliferation of digital technology have revolutionised the way we live, work, and interact. At the forefront of this transformation is the rise of social media platforms, which have woven themselves into the fabric of our daily lives. From the moment we wake up to the time we go to bed, digital interactions shape our experiences, inform our decisions, and influence our emotions.

This book, " Digital Minds: The Psychological Evolution in Enhanced Technology and Social Sites" delves into the profound impact that technology and social media have on our psychological landscape. It explores how our minds are being shaped by the constant connectivity and the curated realities we encounter online. In an age where digital presence is almost as important as physical presence, understanding the psychological ramifications of our online behaviours is crucial.

The Digital Age: A New Era of Human Interaction

In the early days of the internet, the concept of social networking was in its infancy. Platforms like MySpace and Friendster laid the groundwork for what would become a global phenomenon. However, it was the emergence of Facebook in 2004 that truly revolutionised the way we connect with others. With its user-friendly interface and innovative features, Facebook quickly became a central hub for social interaction, setting the stage for other platforms like Twitter, Instagram, and Snapchat to flourish.

Today, social media platforms boast billions of users worldwide. They have become integral to our social lives, professional networks, and even political landscapes. The ability to instantly connect with others, share experiences, and access a vast array of information has transformed society in unprecedented ways.

However, with this transformation comes a host of psychological implications that we are only beginning to understand.

The Psychological Impact of Social Media

One of the most significant aspects of social media is its impact on our psychology. The way we perceive ourselves and others is heavily influenced by the content we consume online. Social media platforms are designed to capture our attention and keep us engaged, often through the use of algorithms that personalise our feeds based on our behaviours and preferences. While this can enhance our user experience, it also creates echo chambers that reinforce our existing beliefs and biases.

Moreover, the curated nature of social media can lead to a distorted view of reality. People tend to share the highlights of their lives, presenting an idealised version of themselves. This can foster feelings of inadequacy, envy, and low self-esteem among users who compare their own lives to these seemingly perfect snapshots. The constant bombardment of information and the pressure to maintain an online presence can also lead to stress, anxiety, and depression.

Understanding Online Behaviour

The field of cyberpsychology seeks to understand how our online behaviours differ from our offline behaviours. The anonymity and distance provided by digital interactions can lead to disinhibition, where individuals feel more comfortable expressing themselves in ways they might not in face-to-face interactions. This can be both positive and negative, fostering open communication and support in some cases, while also leading to cyberbullying and harassment in others.

Furthermore, the impact of social media extends beyond individual psychology to affect group dynamics and societal trends. Social media has the power to mobilise communities, influence public opinion, and drive social change. However, it can also perpetuate misinformation, polarise opinions, and create divisions within society.

The Importance of Digital Well-being

As we navigate this digital landscape, it is essential to consider the concept of digital well-being. This involves being mindful of how technology affects our mental and emotional health and taking steps to mitigate any negative impacts. Practices such as setting boundaries for social media use, engaging in digital detoxes, and fostering real-world connections are crucial for maintaining a healthy relationship with technology.

This book will explore these themes in greater detail, examining the various facets of our digital lives and their psychological implications. From the influence of algorithms on our behaviour to the impact of social media on mental health, we will delve into the complexities of the digital age. By understanding the psychological shifts brought about by enhanced technology and social sites, we can better navigate the challenges and opportunities of this new era.

CHAPTER 1: THE RISE OF SOCIAL MEDIA: A HISTORICAL OVERVIEW

The story of social media is a tale of rapid innovation and widespread adoption. To understand its impact on our psychology, we must first trace its evolution from niche platforms to global giants.

Early Beginnings: From Bulletin Boards to MySpace

The origins of social networking can be traced back to the 1970s and 1980s, with the development of bulletin board systems (BBS) and early online communities like Usenet. These platforms allowed users to share messages and files, fostering a sense of community among tech enthusiasts. However, it wasn't until the late 1990s and early 2000s that social networking began to take its modern form.

One of the first significant social networking sites was SixDegrees.com, launched in 1997. It allowed users to create profiles, list their friends, and connect with others. Although it eventually shut down in 2001, it laid the groundwork for future platforms by demonstrating the potential of social networking.

The Emergence of Friendster and MySpace

In 2002, Friendster was launched, offering a more sophisticated platform for connecting with friends and meeting new people. It quickly gained popularity, attracting millions of users. However, technical issues and competition from other platforms led to its decline.

MySpace, launched in 2003, quickly filled the void left by Friendster. With its customisable profiles, music integration, and strong emphasis on self-expression, MySpace became the most visited website in the United States by 2006. It provided a space for artists, musicians, and ordinary users to showcase their personalities and talents, making it a cultural phenomenon.

The Rise of Facebook

The game-changer in the world of social media came with the launch of Facebook in 2004. Initially restricted to Harvard students, Facebook expanded to other universities and eventually opened its doors to the general public in 2006. Its clean interface, real-name policy, and focus on connecting people in a more personal and authentic way set it apart from its predecessors.

Facebook's success can be attributed to its continuous innovation and ability to adapt to changing user needs. Features like the News Feed, introduced in 2006, and the Like button, introduced in 2009, revolutionised the way people interacted with content and each other. By 2012, Facebook reached one billion active users, cementing its status as the leading social media platform.

The Proliferation of Platforms

Following Facebook's success, numerous other social media platforms emerged, each offering unique features and experiences. Twitter, launched in 2006, introduced the concept of microblogging, allowing users to share short updates and engage in real-time conversations. Instagram, launched in 2010, focused on visual content, enabling users to share photos and videos with filters and effects. Snapchat, launched in 2011, introduced ephemeral messaging, where content disappears after a short period.

These platforms, along with others like LinkedIn, Pinterest, and TikTok, have diversified the social media landscape, catering to different interests and demographics. Each platform has its own unique culture and community, influencing the way users interact and express themselves.

The Mobile Revolution

The widespread adoption of smartphones has further accelerated the growth of social media. With the advent of mobile apps, social media platforms became more accessible and integrated into our daily lives. The ability to connect with others, share content, and stay updated on the go has made social media an indispensable part of modern life.

The Current Landscape

Today, social media platforms boast billions of users worldwide. They have become integral to our social lives, professional networks, and even political landscapes. The ability to instantly connect with others, share experiences, and access a vast array of information has transformed society in unprecedented ways.

The Psychological Implications

As social media continues to evolve, so too does its impact on our psychology. The way we perceive ourselves and others, the way we communicate, and the way we form relationships are all influenced by our online interactions. The curated nature of social media can lead to a distorted view of reality, fostering feelings of inadequacy and envy. The constant bombardment of information and the pressure to maintain an online presence can also lead to stress, anxiety, and depression.

In the following chapters, we will delve deeper into these psychological implications, exploring how social media affects our mental health, self-esteem, and behaviour. By understanding the historical context of social media, we can better appreciate its role in shaping our digital lives and navigate its complexities with greater awareness and resilience.

CHAPTER 2: THE PSYCHOLOGICAL IMPACT OF SOCIAL NETWORKING

Introduction

Social networking has become an integral part of modern life, influencing how we communicate, form relationships, and perceive ourselves and others. As these platforms evolve, so too does their impact on our psychological well-being. This chapter delves into the myriad ways in which social networking affects our mental health, self-esteem, and overall psychological state.

The Allure of Social Media

Social media platforms are designed to capture and maintain our attention. The use of algorithms that tailor content to our preferences creates an engaging and personalised experience. This constant stream of tailored information can be addictive, leading to habitual checking and prolonged usage. The immediate gratification provided by likes, comments, and shares reinforces this behaviour, making it difficult to disconnect.

Positive Psychological Effects

Despite the concerns about social media's impact on mental health, it is important to acknowledge the positive effects it can have:

1. **Social Connectivity**: social media enables people to stay connected with friends and family, regardless of geographical distance. It allows for the maintenance of long-distance relationships and the rekindling of old friendships.

2. **Support Networks**: Online communities provide support for individuals facing similar challenges. From health issues to shared interests, these networks can offer emotional support, advice, and a sense of belonging.

3. **Self-Expression**: Platforms like Instagram, TikTok, and Twitter offer users the opportunity to express themselves creatively. This can boost self-esteem and provide a sense of identity and purpose.

4. **Access to Information**: Social-media serves as a valuable source of news and information. It can raise awareness about social issues, mobilise communities for causes, and provide educational resources.

Negative Psychological Effects

However, the potential negative psychological impacts of social networking are significant and multifaceted:

1. **Social Comparison**: One of the most pervasive issues is social comparison. Users often compare their lives to the idealised versions presented by others online. This can lead to feelings of inadequacy, envy, and low self-esteem.

2. **Anxiety and Depression**: The pressure to maintain an online presence and the fear of missing out (FOMO) can contribute to anxiety and depression. The curated nature of social media feeds, where users predominantly share positive experiences, exacerbates these feelings.

3. **Cyberbullying**: The anonymity and distance provided by social media can lead to cyberbullying. Negative comments, harassment, and public shaming can have severe psychological consequences for victims.

4. **Addiction**: The addictive nature of social media can lead to excessive use, which is associated with negative outcomes such as sleep disturbances, reduced productivity, and impaired real-life relationships.

The Role of Algorithms

Algorithms play a crucial role in shaping our social media experience. They determine what content appears in our feeds based on our past behaviour, likes, and shares. While this can enhance user engagement, it also creates echo chambers where users are exposed predominantly to information that reinforces their existing beliefs. This can lead to polarisation and a skewed perception of reality.

The Impact on Self-Esteem and Body Image

Social media's focus on appearance and lifestyle can have a detrimental effect on self-esteem and body image. Platforms like Instagram and Snapchat, which emphasise visual content, often promote unrealistic beauty standards. The use of filters and photo editing tools can create unattainable ideals, leading users to feel dissatisfied with their own appearance.

Social Media and Mental Health

Numerous studies have explored the link between social media use and mental health. While the results are mixed, there is a growing consensus that excessive social media use is associated with negative mental health outcomes. Symptoms of anxiety, depression, and loneliness are often higher among heavy social media users.

The Role of Cyberpsychology

Cyberpsychology is the study of the psychological impact of technology and online behaviour. This field examines how online interactions differ from offline interactions and the implications for our mental health. Understanding the principles of cyberpsychology can help us develop healthier relationships with technology and social media.

Coping Strategies and Digital Well-being

To mitigate the negative psychological impacts of social networking, it is essential to adopt strategies that promote digital well-being:

1. **Setting Boundaries**: Establishing limits on social media use can help prevent addiction and reduce anxiety. Designating specific times for checking social media and taking regular breaks can be beneficial.

2. **Mindful Consumption**: Being mindful of the content we consume and the accounts we follow can help reduce negative social comparison. Curating a feed that includes positive, inspiring, and diverse perspectives is crucial.

3. **Engaging in Real-Life Activities**: Balancing online interactions with offline activities is important for overall well-

being. Engaging in hobbies, physical exercise, and face-to-face social interactions can provide a healthier balance.

4. **Digital Detox**: Periodically disconnecting from social media, known as a digital detox, can help reset our relationship with technology. This can involve taking short breaks or longer periods of disconnection.

Conclusion

The psychological impact of social networking is complex and multifaceted. While social media offers numerous benefits, including connectivity, support, and self-expression, it also poses significant risks to our mental health and well-being. By understanding these impacts and adopting strategies to mitigate the negative effects, we can navigate the digital landscape with greater awareness and resilience.

In the following chapters, we will explore specific aspects of social media's psychological impact in greater detail, examining the role of algorithms, the influence on mental health, and the importance of digital well-being. By delving deeper into these topics, we aim to provide a comprehensive understanding of how enhanced technology and social sites are reshaping our psychological landscape.

CHAPTER 3: THE ROLE OF ALGORITHMS: SHAPING OUR THOUGHTS AND BEHAVIOURS

Introduction

In the age of social media, algorithms play a pivotal role in determining what content we see and interact with. These sophisticated systems are designed to enhance user experience by personalising content, but they also wield significant influence over our thoughts and behaviours. This chapter explores how algorithms shape our online experiences, the implications for our psychological well-being, and the broader societal impact.

Understanding Algorithms

Algorithms are sets of rules or instructions that computers follow to perform specific tasks. In the context of social media, algorithms analyse user data to predict preferences and interests, thereby curating content to maximise engagement. This data includes past behaviour, such as likes, shares, comments, and time spent on particular posts. By continuously learning from user interactions, algorithms refine their predictions and deliver increasingly personalised content.

Personalisation and Echo Chambers

One of the primary functions of social media algorithms is to personalise the user experience. By prioritising content that aligns with our interests and behaviours, these algorithms create a tailored feed that keeps us engaged. However, this personalisation comes at a cost. It often leads to the formation of echo chambers, where users are predominantly exposed to information that reinforces their existing beliefs and opinions.

The Psychological Impact of Echo Chambers

Echo chambers can have profound psychological effects. When individuals are consistently exposed to content that aligns with their viewpoints, it can lead to confirmation bias, where they become more convinced of their beliefs and less open to opposing perspectives. This can result in increased polarisation and a skewed perception of reality.

The Attention Economy

Social media platforms operate within the attention economy, where user attention is a valuable commodity. Algorithms are designed to maximise the time users spend on the platform by prioritising engaging content. This often includes sensational, emotionally charged, or controversial material, as these types of content are more likely to elicit reactions and keep users hooked.

The Role of Dopamine

The design of social media platforms and their algorithms taps into the brain's reward system. The anticipation of social rewards, such as likes, comments, and shares, triggers the release of dopamine, a neurotransmitter associated with pleasure and reward. This creates a feedback loop, where users repeatedly engage with the platform to experience these rewards, contributing to addictive behaviours.

The Impact on Mental Health

The constant pursuit of social validation through algorithm-driven interactions can have detrimental effects on mental health. The pressure to maintain an idealised online persona, coupled with the fear of missing out (FOMO), can lead to anxiety and depression. Additionally, the exposure to negative or distressing content can exacerbate these conditions.

Manipulation and Misinformation

Algorithms can also be exploited to spread misinformation and manipulate public opinion. The prioritisation of engaging content can amplify sensationalist or misleading information, while the echo chamber effect can insulate users from fact-checking or opposing viewpoints. This has significant implications for democratic processes and societal cohesion.

Case Study: The Cambridge Analytica Scandal

The Cambridge Analytica scandal serves as a stark example of how algorithms can be used to manipulate public opinion. The data analytics firm harvested personal data from millions of Facebook users without their consent and used it to influence voter behaviour in political campaigns. This case highlights the potential for algorithms to be weaponised for political gain and the ethical considerations surrounding data privacy and manipulation.

The Ethical Dilemma

The use of algorithms raises several ethical questions. While personalisation enhances user experience, it also poses risks to privacy, mental health, and social cohesion. Social media companies face the challenge of balancing profit motives with ethical responsibilities to their users and society at large.

Strategies for Mitigating Negative Impacts

To mitigate the negative impacts of algorithms, several strategies can be employed:

1. **Transparency**: Social media companies should provide greater transparency about how their algorithms work and what data is being used. This can help users understand the mechanisms behind their curated feeds and make informed decisions about their online interactions.

2. **Algorithmic Accountability**: There should be accountability mechanisms to ensure that algorithms do not perpetuate harmful behaviours or spread misinformation. Independent audits and regulatory oversight can play a role in holding companies accountable.

3. **User Control**: Giving users more control over their feeds and the content they see can help mitigate the effects of echo chambers. Options to customise algorithms or switch to

chronological feeds can empower users to shape their own online experiences.

4. **Digital Literacy**: Promoting digital literacy is essential in helping users understand the influence of algorithms and develop critical thinking skills. Educational initiatives can equip individuals with the knowledge to navigate the digital landscape more effectively.

5. **Ethical Design**: Social media companies should prioritise ethical design principles that consider the well-being of users. This includes avoiding exploitative practices that maximise engagement at the expense of mental health.

Conclusion

Algorithms are powerful tools that shape our social media experiences, influencing our thoughts, behaviours, and even societal trends. While they offer the promise of personalised content and enhanced user engagement, they also pose significant risks to mental health, social cohesion, and democratic processes. By understanding the role of algorithms and implementing strategies to mitigate their negative impacts, we can navigate the digital world more responsibly and ethically.

In the following chapters, we will continue to explore the psychological implications of enhanced technology and social sites, delving into topics such as cyberpsychology, digital identity, and the impact of social media on mental health. By examining these issues in depth, we aim to provide a comprehensive understanding of the complex interplay between technology and psychology in the digital age.

CHAPTER 4: CYBERPSYCHOLOGY: UNDERSTANDING ONLINE BEHAVIOUR

Introduction

As our lives become increasingly entwined with the digital world, understanding online behaviour has never been more crucial. Cyberpsychology, the study of the impact of technology on human behaviour, provides valuable insights into how we interact with others and perceive ourselves in the virtual realm. This chapter explores the key concepts of cyberpsychology, examining how online environments influence our actions, emotions, and social dynamics.

The Foundations of Cyberpsychology

Cyberpsychology encompasses various psychological principles applied to digital contexts. It examines how traditional psychological theories and concepts translate to online behaviour. This field covers a wide range of topics, including identity formation, social interaction, mental health, and the effects of anonymity.

Digital Identity and Self-Presentation

One of the core areas of cyberpsychology is the study of digital identity. In online environments, individuals have the opportunity to construct and curate their personas more deliberately than in face-to-face interactions. This self-presentation can range from authentic representation to highly edited versions of oneself, influenced by the desire for social approval and the platform's norms.

The Proteus Effect

The Proteus Effect, a concept in cyberpsychology, refers to the phenomenon where the characteristics of an individual's digital avatar influence their behaviour. For instance, users who adopt attractive or authoritative avatars may exhibit more confident and assertive behaviours. This effect highlights the fluidity of identity in digital spaces and the impact of virtual representations on real-world actions.

Social Identity Theory

Social Identity Theory, traditionally applied to offline group dynamics, also plays a role in online interactions. People derive a sense of identity and self-esteem from their membership in various online communities. This can lead to positive outcomes, such as increased social support and belonging, but also negative consequences, such as in-group favouritism and out-group discrimination.

Anonymity and Disinhibition

The anonymity provided by online platforms can significantly alter behaviour. The Online Disinhibition Effect explains how people may behave more freely and aggressively when their actions are not directly linked to their real-world identity. This can lead to both positive outcomes, such as greater openness and self-disclosure, and negative behaviours, such as cyberbullying and trolling.

Positive Disinhibition

Positive disinhibition involves individuals feeling more comfortable sharing personal thoughts and emotions online, which they might withhold in face-to-face interactions. This can lead to greater social support and the formation of deep, meaningful connections.

Negative Disinhibition

Conversely, negative disinhibition manifests as harmful behaviours, including rudeness, aggression, and harassment. The perceived lack of consequences and the psychological distance from the target contribute to this phenomenon. Cyberbullying, in particular, is a significant concern, with severe psychological impacts on victims.

Online Relationships

The nature of relationships formed online can differ markedly from those in the offline world. Cyberpsychology explores how these relationships develop, the dynamics involved, and their implications for mental health and well-being.

Friendships and Social Support

Online friendships can provide substantial social support, particularly for individuals who may feel isolated or marginalised in their offline lives. Digital platforms enable people to find like-minded communities and build connections based on shared interests and experiences.

Romantic Relationships

The digital age has transformed romantic relationships, with online dating becoming increasingly common. Cyberpsychology examines how these relationships are initiated, maintained, and sometimes terminated. While online dating offers opportunities for connection, it also presents challenges, such as the potential for deception and the impact of digital communication on intimacy.

The Impact of Social Media on Behaviour

Social media platforms are central to the study of cyberpsychology, as they profoundly influence our behaviour and social interactions. Key areas of focus include the effects of social media on self-esteem, social comparison, and mental health.

Social Comparison

Social comparison theory suggests that individuals evaluate their own worth by comparing themselves to others. Social media amplifies this behaviour, as users are constantly exposed to curated, idealised representations of others' lives. This can lead to feelings of inadequacy and decreased self-esteem.

Fear of Missing Out (FOMO)

FOMO is a phenomenon exacerbated by social media, where individuals feel anxiety over the possibility of missing out on rewarding experiences that others are having. This can lead to compulsive checking of social media and an inability to disconnect, contributing to stress and dissatisfaction.

Mental Health Implications

The impact of social media on mental health is a significant concern in cyberpsychology. While it can offer social support and connectivity, excessive use and negative interactions can lead to anxiety, depression, and other mental health issues. The pressure to present a perfect life online and the constant exposure to others' highlights can contribute to these adverse outcomes.

Cyberpsychology in the Workplace

The principles of cyberpsychology are also relevant in professional settings, where technology and online communication are integral. Understanding how digital interactions influence workplace behaviour and dynamics can improve productivity, job satisfaction, and mental health.

Remote Working

The rise of remote working has brought new challenges and opportunities for workplace psychology. Cyberpsychology explores how virtual collaboration tools, digital communication, and the blurring of work-life boundaries affect employee well-being and performance.

Online Professional Identity

Just as individuals curate their personal identities online, they also manage their professional personas. LinkedIn and other professional networks play a crucial role in career development, networking, and job searching. Understanding the impact of these platforms on professional behaviour and identity is an emerging area of interest.

Conclusion

Cyberpsychology provides a comprehensive framework for understanding the complex interplay between human behaviour and digital environments. By examining how online contexts influence our actions, emotions, and social interactions, we can develop strategies to navigate the digital world more effectively and promote mental well-being.

In the following chapters, we will delve deeper into specific aspects of cyberpsychology, such as the impact of technology on mental health, the role of digital identity, and the influence of social media on self-esteem and body image. By exploring these topics, we aim to provide a nuanced understanding of the psychological shifts brought about by enhanced technology and social sites.

CHAPTER 5: THE IMPACT OF TECHNOLOGY ON MENTAL HEALTH

Introduction

Technology has revolutionised our lives, offering unprecedented convenience, connectivity, and access to information. However, the rapid integration of technology into daily life has also raised concerns about its impact on mental health. This chapter explores how various forms of technology, including smartphones, social media, and the internet, influence our mental well-being, highlighting both the positive and negative effects.

The Double-Edged Sword of Technology

Technology serves as a double-edged sword, providing numerous benefits while also posing potential risks to mental health. Understanding this dual nature is crucial for navigating the digital landscape responsibly and maintaining mental well-being.

Positive Impacts of Technology on Mental Health

Despite the concerns, technology offers several positive impacts on mental health:

1. **Access to Information and Resources**: The internet provides vast resources for mental health education and support. Individuals can access information on various mental health conditions, treatment options, and self-help strategies, empowering them to take control of their mental health.

2. **Online Therapy and Support Groups**: Technology has made mental health services more accessible through online therapy platforms and support groups. These services offer

convenience, anonymity, and a broader reach, especially for those who may have difficulty accessing traditional in-person services.

3. **Mental Health Apps**: There are numerous apps designed to support mental health, offering tools for meditation, mindfulness, mood tracking, and cognitive behavioural therapy (CBT). These apps can help users manage stress, anxiety, and depression.

4. **Social Connectivity**: Social-media and messaging platforms enable people to stay connected with friends and family, reducing feelings of loneliness and isolation. These connections can provide emotional support and a sense of community.

Negative Impacts of Technology on Mental Health

Conversely, the negative impacts of technology on mental health are significant and multifaceted:

1. **Screen Time and Sleep Disruption**: Excessive screen time, particularly before bed, can disrupt sleep patterns, leading to insomnia and poor sleep quality. The blue light emitted by screens interferes with the production of melatonin, a hormone that regulates sleep.

2. **Social-Media and Mental Health**: While social media can enhance connectivity, it also has drawbacks. Social comparison, cyberbullying, and the pressure to maintain an idealised online persona can lead to anxiety, depression, and low self-esteem.

3. **Digital Addiction**: The addictive nature of technology, particularly smartphones and social media, can lead to compulsive use. This can result in decreased productivity, impaired real-life relationships, and increased stress and anxiety.

4. **Information Overload**: The constant influx of information from digital sources can be overwhelming, leading to cognitive overload and stress. The pressure to stay updated and the fear of missing out (FOMO) can exacerbate these feelings.

The Role of Smartphones

Smartphones are ubiquitous in modern life, serving as essential tools for communication, work, and entertainment. However, their pervasive presence has raised concerns about their impact on mental health.

Smartphone Addiction

Smartphone addiction, characterised by excessive and compulsive use, can lead to negative mental health outcomes. Symptoms include anxiety, irritability, and difficulty concentrating when the device is not accessible. The constant need to check notifications and stay connected can create a cycle of dependency.

Social Media and Anxiety

Social media platforms, accessed primarily through smartphones, are significant contributors to anxiety. The pressure to keep up with social interactions, maintain an idealised image, and receive validation through likes and comments can create a stressful environment. Additionally, exposure to distressing news and cyberbullying further exacerbates anxiety levels.

The Internet and Mental Health

The internet, while a valuable resource, also presents challenges for mental health:

Cyberbullying

Cyberbullying is a pervasive issue on the internet, with severe psychological consequences for victims. The anonymity and reach of online platforms allow bullies to target individuals without facing immediate repercussions. Victims of cyberbullying often experience anxiety, depression, and low self-esteem.

Online Communities

Online communities can provide support and a sense of belonging, especially for individuals with shared interests or experiences. However, they can also reinforce negative behaviours and beliefs, particularly in forums that promote harmful activities or ideologies.

Exposure to Negative Content

The internet exposes users to a wide range of content, some of which can be distressing. Exposure to graphic images, violent news, and negative social interactions can contribute to anxiety, depression, and trauma.

Managing the Impact of Technology on Mental Health

To mitigate the negative impacts of technology on mental health, it is essential to adopt strategies that promote healthy digital habits:

1. **Setting Boundaries**: Establishing clear boundaries for technology use, such as designated screen-free times and areas, can help reduce dependency and improve mental well-being.

2. **Digital Detox**: Periodically disconnecting from digital devices, known as a digital detox, can help reset our relationship with technology and reduce stress.

3. **Mindful Use of Social-Media**: Being mindful of how and why we use social media can help mitigate its negative effects. Limiting time spent on social media, curating a positive feed, and engaging in meaningful interactions are crucial steps.

4. **Prioritising Real-Life Interactions**: Balancing online interactions with face-to-face social connections is essential for mental health. Engaging in real-life activities and maintaining strong offline relationships can provide emotional support and fulfilment.

5. **Healthy Sleep Habits**: Reducing screen time before bed and creating a relaxing bedtime routine can improve sleep quality. Using features like blue light filters on devices can also help mitigate the impact on sleep.

6. **Utilising Technology for Mental Health**: Leveraging technology's positive aspects, such as mental health apps and online therapy, can provide valuable support and resources.

Conclusion

Technology's impact on mental health is complex, offering both significant benefits and substantial risks. By understanding these effects and adopting strategies to promote healthy digital habits, we can harness technology's potential while mitigating its adverse impacts on mental well-being.

In the following chapters, we will further explore specific aspects of the digital age's psychological landscape, such as the influence of social media on self-esteem and body image, the ethical implications of algorithmic manipulation, and strategies for fostering digital well-being. Through this comprehensive exploration, we aim to equip readers with the knowledge and tools to navigate the digital world responsibly and maintain mental health in the face of technological advancements.

CHAPTER 6: DIGITAL IDENTITY: CRAFTING PERSONAS ONLINE

Introduction

In the digital age, identity has taken on a new dimension. The advent of social media, virtual communities, and online platforms has allowed individuals to craft digital personas that may or may not reflect their real-world selves. This chapter delves into the concept of digital identity, exploring how and why people create these online personas, the psychological implications, and the impact on personal and social dynamics.

The Concept of Digital Identity

Digital identity refers to the way individuals present themselves in the online world. Unlike the fixed and often constrained identity we exhibit in face-to-face interactions, digital identity is fluid and malleable, allowing for creative self-expression and the exploration of different facets of one's personality.

Motivations for Crafting Digital Personas

The reasons behind crafting digital personas are varied and complex. Some of the primary motivations include:

1. **Self-Expression**: The internet provides a platform for individuals to express aspects of their identity that may not be visible in their offline lives. This includes artistic talents, unique interests, and personal viewpoints.

2. **Social Approval**: Many users curate their online personas to seek validation and approval from others. The pursuit of likes, comments, and followers can drive individuals to present idealised versions of themselves.

3. **Anonymity and Freedom**: The relative anonymity of the internet allows people to explore and express parts of their identity without fear of judgment or repercussions. This can be liberating for those who feel constrained by societal norms.

4. **Professional Advancement**: In professional contexts, individuals often craft their digital personas to enhance their

careers. This includes maintaining a professional presence on platforms like LinkedIn and showcasing expertise in their field.

5. **Connection and Belonging**: Online personas help individuals connect with like-minded communities. By presenting themselves in a certain way, they can attract and engage with others who share their interests and values.

The Mechanics of Digital Identity

Creating and maintaining a digital identity involves several key elements:

1. **Profile Information**: This includes basic information such as name, age, location, and occupation. Users often embellish or selectively disclose this information to craft a particular image.

2. **Content Creation**: The photos, videos, posts, and stories shared online are central to digital identity. These elements are carefully curated to align with the desired persona.

3. **Interaction Patterns**: The way individuals interact with others online—through comments, likes, shares, and direct messages—also shapes their digital identity. These interactions can reinforce the persona they wish to project.

4. **Visual Aesthetics**: The visual presentation of profiles, including themes, colour schemes, and overall aesthetics, plays a significant role in digital identity. Platforms like Instagram and Pinterest emphasise visual appeal.

The Fluidity of Digital Identity

Unlike offline identity, which is often constrained by social roles and expectations, digital identity is inherently fluid. Individuals can experiment with different aspects of their personality and adjust their online personas based on feedback and changing preferences. This fluidity allows for continuous self-reinvention and adaptation.

Psychological Implications of Digital Identity

The creation and maintenance of digital identities have several psychological implications:

1. **Self-Esteem and Validation**: The pursuit of social approval online can significantly impact self-esteem. Positive feedback can boost self-confidence, while negative comments or lack of engagement can lead to feelings of inadequacy.

2. **Identity Exploration and Development**: The internet provides a space for identity exploration, particularly for adolescents and young adults. This can be a critical part of personal development, allowing individuals to experiment with different identities and find their authentic selves.

3. **Cognitive Dissonance**: When there is a significant disparity between one's online persona and real-world identity, it can lead to cognitive dissonance. This internal conflict can cause stress and anxiety.

4. **Privacy and Boundaries**: Balancing transparency and privacy is a key challenge in crafting digital identities. Oversharing can lead to privacy breaches, while under-sharing may result in a less engaging online presence.

Case Studies: Digital Identity in Action

Influencers and Content Creators

Influencers and content creators exemplify the power and complexity of digital identity. Their success often hinges on their ability to craft relatable, aspirational, and engaging personas. They invest considerable effort into curating content that aligns with their brand and resonates with their audience. The pressures of maintaining such personas can, however, lead to burnout and identity crises.

Online Dating Profiles

In the realm of online dating, digital identity plays a crucial role. Users craft profiles that highlight their most attractive qualities and interests to attract potential partners. The challenge lies in balancing authenticity with the desire to present an appealing persona. Misrepresentation can lead to disappointment and mistrust when online interactions transition to the real world.

Professional Networks

Platforms like LinkedIn demonstrate the strategic crafting of professional personas. Users present their skills, achievements, and professional experiences in a way that enhances their career prospects. Maintaining a consistent and professional digital identity is essential for networking and job opportunities.

The Impact on Personal and Social Dynamics

Digital identities influence not only individual psychology but also broader social dynamics:

1. **Authenticity and Trust**: The discrepancy between online personas and real-world identities can affect trust in digital interactions. Authenticity is highly valued, and perceived inauthenticity can lead to scepticism and distrust.

2. **Social Comparison**: The idealised portrayals of life on social media can lead to negative social comparison. Users may feel inadequate when comparing their real lives to the seemingly perfect lives of others online.

3. **Community and Belonging**: Digital identities enable individuals to find and connect with communities that share their interests and values. These connections can provide a sense of belonging and support, particularly for those who feel isolated offline.

4. **Cultural and Societal Influence**: Digital identities contribute to cultural and societal trends. Influencers, in particular, can shape public opinion, fashion, and lifestyle choices through their online personas.

Strategies for Healthy Digital Identity Management

To navigate the complexities of digital identity, it is essential to adopt strategies that promote authenticity and well-being:

1. **Mindful Self-Presentation**: Being mindful of how and why we present ourselves online can help ensure our digital personas align with our true selves. Reflecting on the motivations behind our online behaviour can promote authenticity.

2. **Balancing Transparency and Privacy**: Finding a balance between sharing and privacy is crucial. It is important to be selective about what personal information is shared and to set boundaries to protect privacy.

3. **Positive Engagement**: Engaging positively with others online, avoiding negative interactions, and seeking supportive communities can enhance the digital experience. Constructive feedback and genuine connections contribute to a healthier digital identity.

4. **Digital Detox and Real-World Interaction**: Taking breaks from digital platforms and prioritising real-world interactions can help maintain a balanced perspective. Face-to-face relationships and offline activities provide grounding and prevent over-reliance on digital validation.

5. **Critical Media Literacy**: Developing critical media literacy skills enables individuals to navigate digital content more effectively. Understanding the mechanisms behind social media algorithms and the curated nature of online content can reduce the impact of social comparison and misinformation.

Conclusion

Crafting digital identities is an integral part of the modern digital landscape. While these personas offer opportunities for self-expression, connection, and professional advancement, they also present challenges related to authenticity, privacy, and mental health. By understanding the motivations behind digital identity and adopting strategies for healthy management, individuals can navigate the digital world with greater confidence and well-being.

In the following chapters, we will continue to explore the psychological dimensions of technology and social media, delving into topics such as the influence of social media on self-esteem and body image, the ethical considerations of algorithmic manipulation, and the development of digital resilience. Through this comprehensive examination, we aim to provide insights and tools to foster a healthier relationship with technology and digital identities.

CHAPTER 7: THE INFLUENCE OF SOCIAL MEDIA ON SELF-ESTEEM AND BODY IMAGE

Introduction

In today's digitally interconnected world, social media has become a ubiquitous part of daily life. Platforms like Instagram, Facebook, and TikTok allow users to share moments, connect with others, and engage in various forms of self-expression. While these platforms offer numerous benefits, they also present significant challenges, particularly concerning self-esteem and body image. This chapter explores the complex relationship between social media, self-esteem, and body image, examining both the positive and negative impacts.

The Role of Social Media in Shaping Self-Esteem

Self-esteem, defined as an individual's overall sense of self-worth or personal value, can be significantly influenced by social media interactions. The constant exposure to idealised representations of life and beauty on these platforms often leads to social comparison, where individuals evaluate themselves against the images and lifestyles portrayed by others. This can have several effects:

1. **Positive Reinforcement**: Receiving likes, comments, and followers can boost self-esteem, providing validation and a sense of belonging. Positive interactions can reinforce a positive self-image and enhance social connections.

2. **Negative Comparison**: Conversely, seeing others' seemingly perfect lives and appearances can lead to feelings of inadequacy and lowered self-esteem. This is especially pronounced when users compare themselves to influencers and celebrities who often present an edited, idealised version of reality.

3. **Feedback and Validation**: The feedback loop on social media, where users seek and receive validation through engagement metrics, can create a dependency on external approval. This can lead to fluctuating self-esteem, heavily influenced by online interactions.

4. **Cyberbullying and Harassment**: Negative interactions, such as cyberbullying and online harassment, can severely damage self-esteem. Victims of online abuse may experience increased anxiety, depression, and a diminished sense of self-worth.

The Impact of Social Media on Body Image

Body image, or how one perceives their physical appearance, is another area profoundly affected by social media. The prevalence of edited, filtered, and often unrealistic images on social media can distort perceptions of beauty and body standards. The impact includes:

1. **Idealised Beauty Standards**: social media perpetuates narrow beauty ideals, often unattainable without digital enhancement. This can lead individuals to strive for unrealistic body types and appearances, fostering dissatisfaction with their own bodies.

2. **Body Dysmorphia**: Continuous exposure to idealised images can contribute to body dysmorphic disorder (BDD), where individuals obsess over perceived flaws in their appearance. This can lead to unhealthy behaviours such as extreme dieting, excessive exercise, and cosmetic surgery.

3. **Eating disorders**: The pressure to conform to ideal body standards can also trigger or exacerbate eating disorders like anorexia, bulimia, and binge-eating disorder. Social media platforms, particularly those focused on visual content, often glorify thinness and fitness, perpetuating harmful stereotypes and behaviours.

4. **Positive Body Image Movements**: Despite these challenges, social media also hosts positive body image movements, promoting body positivity and self-acceptance. Campaigns that celebrate diverse body types and challenge traditional beauty norms can provide support and empowerment to users.

Case Studies and Research Findings

Several studies have examined the link between social media usage and its effects on self-esteem and body image. Key findings include:

1. **Adolescents and Young Adults**: Research indicates that adolescents and young adults are particularly vulnerable to the negative impacts of social media on self-esteem and body image. This demographic is often in the process of identity formation and is highly sensitive to peer validation and social comparison.

2. **Gender Differences**: Studies show that women are more likely than men to be affected by body image issues related to social media. However, men are not immune, with increasing pressure to conform to ideals of muscularity and fitness.

3. **Influence of Influencers**: Influencers play a significant role in shaping perceptions of beauty and lifestyle. Their curated content often sets unattainable standards, contributing to feelings

of inadequacy among followers. However, influencers who promote authenticity and body positivity can have a positive impact.

4. **Mental Health Correlation**: There is a strong correlation between excessive social media use and mental health issues such as anxiety, depression, and low self-esteem. The constant comparison and the need for validation can exacerbate these conditions.

Strategies for Mitigating Negative Effects

To navigate the complex landscape of social media, several strategies can help mitigate its negative impacts on self-esteem and body image:

1. **Media Literacy Education**: Educating users, particularly young people, about the constructed nature of social media content can foster critical thinking and reduce the impact of unrealistic comparisons.

2. **Promoting Authenticity**: Encouraging authenticity and transparency among social media users and influencers can help create a more realistic and inclusive online environment. Celebrating diverse body types and lifestyles can counteract the harmful effects of idealised portrayals.

3. **Mindful Social Media Use**: Practising mindful social media use, such as setting time limits, curating a positive feed, and engaging in offline activities, can reduce dependency on online validation and promote a healthier self-image.

4. **Support Networks**: Building and maintaining supportive offline relationships can provide a buffer against the negative impacts of social media. Family, friends, and professional support can offer perspective and encouragement.

5. **Mental Health Resources**: Access to mental health resources, including counselling and support groups, can help individuals struggling with self-esteem and body image issues exacerbated by social media.

Conclusion

The influence of social media on self-esteem and body image is multifaceted and significant. While social media offers platforms for connection and self-expression, it also presents challenges related to social comparison and unrealistic beauty standards. By understanding these dynamics and employing strategies to mitigate negative effects, users can navigate social media in a way that promotes self-acceptance and mental well-being.

In the following chapters, we will continue to explore the psychological dimensions of technology and social media, addressing topics such as the ethical considerations of data privacy, the impact of virtual reality on human perception, and the development of digital resilience. Through this comprehensive examination, we aim to provide insights and tools to foster a healthier relationship with technology and digital identities.

CHAPTER 8: THE SOCIAL COMPARISON THEORY IN THE DIGITAL AGE

Introduction

Social comparison theory, originally proposed by psychologist Leon Festinger in 1954, posits that individuals determine their own social and personal worth based on how they stack up against others. Historically, these comparisons occurred within local communities and immediate social circles. However, the advent of the digital age and the rise of social media platforms have transformed the landscape of social comparison, making it more pervasive and impactful. This chapter delves into the dynamics of social comparison theory in the context of the digital age, exploring how technology amplifies these comparisons and their psychological consequences.

The Fundamentals of Social Comparison Theory

Social comparison theory suggests that people have an inherent drive to evaluate themselves, often in relation to others. These comparisons can be upward (comparing oneself to someone perceived as better) or downward (comparing oneself to someone perceived as worse). Both types of comparison can have distinct psychological effects:

1. **Upward Comparison**: While this can serve as motivation for self-improvement, it can also lead to feelings of inadequacy, lower self-esteem, and anxiety if the comparisons seem unattainable.

2. **Downward Comparison**: This can boost self-esteem and provide a sense of relief but may also foster complacency and a lack of motivation to improve.

Digital Amplification of Social Comparison

In the digital age, social comparison has been amplified by several factors:

1. **Accessibility and Ubiquity**: Social media platforms provide constant access to others' lives, enabling continuous comparisons. The ubiquity of smartphones ensures that users are almost always connected, heightening the frequency of these comparisons.

2. **Curated Content**: Social media profiles often showcase curated, idealised versions of users' lives. This selective self-presentation can lead to skewed perceptions of reality, making upward comparisons more likely and more damaging.

3. **Quantifiable Metrics**: Likes, comments, followers, and other engagement metrics provide tangible indicators of social approval, turning social validation into a numerical value. This

can exacerbate feelings of inadequacy or superiority based on these metrics.

4. **Algorithmic Influence**: Algorithms on social media platforms often amplify content that is engaging or provocative, which can increase exposure to idealised lifestyles and appearances, reinforcing social comparison.

Psychological Consequences of Digital Social Comparison

The pervasive nature of social comparison in the digital age has several psychological consequences:

1. **Impaired Self-Esteem**: Frequent upward comparisons can lead to chronic dissatisfaction with oneself, negatively impacting self-esteem. Users may feel inadequate when comparing their own lives to the seemingly perfect lives of others.

2. **Anxiety and Depression**: The pressure to meet unrealistic standards set by social media can contribute to anxiety and depression. This is particularly pronounced in adolescents and young adults who are still developing their identities.

3. **Body Image Issues**: As discussed in the previous chapter, social media perpetuates idealised body standards, leading to body dissatisfaction and related issues such as eating disorders and body dysmorphic disorder.

4. **FOMO (Fear of Missing Out)**: Constant exposure to others' social activities can create a sense of missing out on life experiences, leading to feelings of loneliness and social anxiety.

5. **Perfectionism**: The desire to present a perfect image online can drive unhealthy perfectionism, where individuals strive for unattainable standards, leading to stress and burnout.

Case Studies and Research Findings

Research and case studies provide valuable insights into the impact of digital social comparison:

1. **Adolescent Vulnerability**: Studies have shown that adolescents, who are highly active on social media, are particularly vulnerable to negative effects of social comparison. Their self-esteem and body image can be significantly impacted by the content they consume.

2. **Gender Differences**: Research indicates that while both men and women engage in social comparison, the nature and impact can differ. Women often compare physical appearance, leading to body dissatisfaction, whereas men may focus on achievements and status.

3. **Influence of Influencers**: Influencers set trends and standards that followers often aspire to. However, the gap between the curated lives of influencers and the realities of their followers can lead to significant social comparison stress.

4. **Cultural Variations**: The impact of social comparison can vary across cultures. In collectivist societies, where group harmony and social cohesion are valued, social comparison may have different implications compared to individualist societies, where personal achievement and individualism are emphasised.

Strategies for Mitigating Negative Effects

To combat the negative effects of social comparison in the digital age, several strategies can be employed:

1. **Digital Literacy Education**: Teaching users, especially young people, to critically evaluate social media content can reduce the impact of unrealistic comparisons. Understanding that social media often represents curated and edited versions of reality can help mitigate feelings of inadequacy.

2. **Encouraging Authenticity**: Promoting authenticity and realistic portrayals on social media can create a healthier environment. Encouraging users to share both successes and struggles can foster a more supportive and realistic community.

3. **Mindful Social Media Use**: Practising mindful social media use, such as setting limits on screen time, curating a

positive feed, and engaging with content that promotes well-being, can reduce the frequency and impact of negative comparisons.

4. **Fostering Offline Relationships**: Building strong offline relationships can provide a buffer against the negative impacts of online social comparison. Face-to-face interactions can offer more authentic validation and support.

5. **Mental Health Support**: Providing access to mental health resources and support can help individuals cope with the psychological stress caused by social comparison. Counselling, support groups, and mental health education can offer valuable tools for managing these challenges.

Conclusion

The digital age has profoundly transformed the dynamics of social comparison, making it a pervasive aspect of modern life. While social media offers platforms for connection and self-expression, it also amplifies the tendency to compare oneself to others, often with detrimental effects on self-esteem, mental health, and body image. By understanding the mechanisms of social comparison and employing strategies to mitigate its negative impacts, individuals can navigate the digital landscape more healthily and positively.

In the next chapter, we will explore the ethical considerations surrounding data privacy in the digital age, examining how personal data is collected, used, and protected in an increasingly interconnected world. Through this exploration, we aim to provide insights into maintaining privacy and security while engaging with digital technologies.

CHAPTER 9: ONLINE RELATIONSHIPS: FRIENDSHIP, ROMANCE, AND COMMUNITY

Introduction

In the digital age, the nature of human relationships has evolved dramatically. The internet and social media platforms have created new avenues for forming and maintaining connections. Online relationships, encompassing friendships, romantic partnerships, and community memberships, have become integral to modern social life. This chapter explores the dynamics of online relationships, their benefits and challenges, and the impact they have on our social and emotional well-being.

Online Friendships

Online friendships are increasingly common, facilitated by social media, forums, and gaming platforms. These digital connections often transcend geographical boundaries, bringing together individuals with shared interests and experiences.

1. **Formation of Online Friendships**: Online friendships typically begin in virtual spaces where individuals share common interests, such as fan communities, gaming platforms, or professional networks. These shared spaces provide a foundation for initial interactions and the development of deeper connections.

2. **Benefits of Online Friendships**:

   - **Diverse Perspectives**: Online friendships often connect people from different cultural backgrounds, providing exposure to diverse perspectives and experiences.

   - **Support Networks**: Digital friends can offer significant emotional support, especially for individuals who may feel isolated in their offline lives.

   - **Convenience and Accessibility**: Online communication tools make it easy to maintain friendships regardless of physical distance, allowing for real-time interactions and continuous engagement.

3. **Challenges of Online Friendships**:

   - **Lack of Physical Presence**: The absence of physical interaction can sometimes make it difficult to fully gauge the depth of the relationship or provide tangible support.

   - **Trust and Authenticity**: Building trust in online friendships can be challenging due to the potential for misrepresentation or deception.

   - **Screen Dependency**: Excessive reliance on digital communication can sometimes detract from offline social interactions and experiences.

Online Romantic Relationships

Romantic relationships that begin and develop online have become increasingly common, thanks to dating apps and social media platforms. These relationships offer unique opportunities and challenges.

1. **Initiation of Online Romances**: Dating apps like Tinder, Bumble, and OkCupid facilitate the formation of romantic relationships by matching individuals based on preferences and interests. Social media platforms also serve as venues for romantic interactions.

2. **Benefits of Online Romantic Relationships**:

   - **Expanded Pool of Partners**: Online dating expands the pool of potential partners beyond one's immediate geographic area, increasing the chances of finding a compatible match.

   - **Convenience**: Online communication allows couples to maintain contact easily, regardless of physical distance.

   - **Focus on Compatibility**: Many dating apps use algorithms to match individuals based on compatibility factors, potentially leading to more fulfilling relationships.

3. **Challenges of Online Romantic Relationships**:

   - **Misrepresentation**: The potential for individuals to misrepresent themselves online can lead to mismatched expectations and disappointment.

   - **Long-Distance Struggles**: Maintaining a romantic relationship over long distances can be challenging, requiring significant effort and commitment from both parties.

   - **Emotional Risks**: The emotional intensity of online romances can sometimes lead to heightened vulnerability and potential heartbreak.

Online Communities

Online communities, whether based on shared interests, professions, or support needs, play a crucial role in the digital age. These communities provide a sense of belonging and a platform for collective engagement.

1. **Formation and Functioning of Online Communities**: Online communities form around common interests or goals, such as fan groups, professional networks, or support groups. Platforms like Reddit, Facebook Groups, and specialized forums facilitate the creation and maintenance of these communities.

2. **Benefits of Online Communities**:

- **Support and Solidarity**: Online communities offer support and solidarity, particularly for individuals facing similar challenges or pursuing common interests.

   - **Knowledge Sharing**: These communities provide a space for sharing knowledge and experiences, fostering learning and growth.

   - **Activism and Advocacy**: Online communities can mobilize collective action for social causes, raising awareness and advocating for change.

3. **Challenges of Online Communities**:

   - **Echo Chambers**: Online communities can sometimes become echo chambers, reinforcing existing beliefs and limiting exposure to diverse perspectives.

   - **Toxicity and Harassment**: The anonymity of online interactions can lead to toxic behaviour and harassment, detracting from the positive aspects of the community.

   - **Maintaining Engagement**: Keeping members engaged and active in the community can be challenging, requiring effective moderation and management.

 Psychological and Emotional Impact

The psychological and emotional impact of online relationships varies, influenced by factors such as the nature of the relationship, the platform used, and individual differences.

1. **Positive Impacts**:

   - **Enhanced Social Support**: Online relationships can provide substantial social support, enhancing emotional well-being and reducing feelings of loneliness.

   - **Increased Self-Expression**: Digital platforms allow for diverse forms of self-expression, enabling individuals to connect with others who appreciate their unique perspectives.

- **Personal Growth**: Engaging with diverse online communities can foster personal growth and broaden one's horizons.

2. **Negative Impacts**:

   - **Emotional Vulnerability**: The intensity of online relationships can sometimes lead to emotional vulnerability and distress, especially in cases of deception or rejection.

   - **Dependence on Digital Validation**: Excessive reliance on online relationships for validation can negatively impact self-esteem and mental health.

   - **Social Isolation**: While online relationships can provide support, they may also contribute to social isolation if they replace offline interactions.

Strategies for Healthy Online Relationships

To navigate online relationships effectively and mitigate potential negative impacts, several strategies can be employed:

1. **Balancing Online and Offline Interactions**: Striking a balance between online and offline interactions is crucial for maintaining healthy relationships and overall well-being.

2. **Practicing Digital Literacy**: Developing digital literacy skills, including critical thinking and awareness of online risks, can help individuals navigate online relationships more safely and effectively.

3. **Setting Boundaries**: Establishing clear boundaries in online relationships can prevent overdependence and protect emotional well-being.

4. **Building Trust**: Taking the time to build trust and authenticity in online relationships can enhance their quality and sustainability.

5. **Seeking Support**: Accessing mental health resources and support networks can help individuals cope with the emotional challenges of online relationships.

Conclusion

Online relationships, encompassing friendships, romantic partnerships, and community memberships, have become integral to modern social life. While they offer numerous benefits, including expanded social networks and enhanced support, they also present unique challenges. By understanding the dynamics of online relationships and employing strategies to navigate them effectively, individuals can foster meaningful connections and enhance their overall well-being.

In the following chapters, we will continue to explore the psychological dimensions of technology and social media, addressing topics such as the ethical considerations of data privacy, the impact of virtual reality on human perception, and the development of digital resilience. Through this comprehensive examination, we aim to provide insights and tools to foster a healthier relationship with technology and digital identities.

CHAPTER 10: DIGITAL DETOX: THE NEED FOR A BREAK FROM TECHNOLOGY

Introduction

In the fast-paced, always-connected world of today, technology permeates almost every aspect of our lives. While the digital age brings numerous benefits, including instant communication, access to vast information, and innovative tools, it also comes with drawbacks. Constant connectivity can lead to burnout, stress, and a host of physical and mental health issues. This chapter explores the concept of a digital detox, the necessity for periodic breaks from technology, and practical strategies to implement these breaks for better well-being.

Understanding Digital Detox

A digital detox refers to a period during which an individual refrains from using digital devices such as smartphones, computers, tablets, and social media platforms. The goal is to reduce stress, improve mental health, and reconnect with the physical world. The practice of taking a break from digital engagement is becoming increasingly important as more people recognise the adverse effects of constant connectivity.

The Psychological Impact of Constant Connectivity

1. **Mental Fatigue**: Continuous exposure to digital information can lead to mental overload. The brain is constantly processing data, which can result in cognitive fatigue and decreased attention span.

2. **Stress and Anxiety**: Social media platforms often contribute to stress and anxiety. The pressure to stay updated, fear of missing out (FOMO), and the comparison with others' curated lives can exacerbate these feelings.

3. **Sleep Disruption**: The blue light emitted by screens interferes with the production of melatonin, a hormone that regulates sleep. This can lead to sleep disturbances and negatively impact overall health.

4. **Reduced Productivity**: Multitasking with digital devices can decrease productivity. Constant notifications and the temptation to check social media can disrupt focus and reduce work efficiency.

5. **Emotional Well-Being**: The emotional ups and downs triggered by social media interactions, such as likes, comments, and shares, can affect self-esteem and emotional stability.

Physical Health Concerns

1. **Eye Strain**: Prolonged screen time can cause digital eye strain, leading to discomfort, headaches, and vision problems.

2. **Sedentary Lifestyle**: Excessive use of digital devices often results in a sedentary lifestyle, contributing to various health issues such as obesity, cardiovascular disease, and musculoskeletal problems.

3. **Posture Problems**: Poor posture while using devices can lead to neck, back, and shoulder pain, commonly referred to as "tech neck."

Benefits of a Digital Detox

Taking a break from technology can yield several positive outcomes:

1. **Improved Mental Health**: Reducing screen time can lower stress levels, improve mood, and increase overall mental well-being.

2. **Enhanced Sleep Quality**: Limiting exposure to screens, especially before bedtime, can improve sleep quality and duration.

3. **Better Focus and Productivity**: A digital detox can help regain focus, enhance concentration, and boost productivity by eliminating constant distractions.

4. **Stronger Personal Connections**: Disconnecting from digital devices can lead to more meaningful interactions with family and friends, strengthening personal relationships.

5. **Physical Health Benefits**: Reduced screen time encourages a more active lifestyle, alleviates eye strain, and improves posture.

Strategies for Implementing a Digital Detox

1. **Set Clear Goals**: Determine the purpose of your digital detox and set specific, achievable goals. This could include

reducing overall screen time, avoiding social media, or unplugging during certain hours of the day.

2. **Create a Schedule**: Plan your digital detox in advance. Decide on the duration and frequency of your breaks from technology. This could be a daily break, a weekend without screens, or a longer retreat.

3. **Inform Others**: Let friends, family, and colleagues know about your digital detox plans. This will help manage expectations and reduce pressure to respond immediately.

4. **Find Alternatives**: Identify activities that can replace digital consumption. This could include reading a book, exercising, spending time outdoors, or engaging in hobbies.

5. **Use Technology to Your Advantage**: There are apps designed to help manage screen time and encourage digital detoxing. Use these tools to track usage and set limits.

6. **Establish No-Tech Zones**: Designate certain areas in your home, such as the bedroom or dining area, as no-tech zones to promote healthier habits.

7. **Practice Mindfulness**: Engage in mindfulness activities such as meditation or yoga to reconnect with yourself and reduce the impulse to reach for digital devices.

Case Studies and Success Stories

Numerous individuals and organisations have successfully implemented digital detox practices with positive outcomes. For instance:

1. **Corporate Digital Detox Programs**: Some companies have introduced digital detox initiatives for their employees, resulting in improved morale, productivity, and job satisfaction. These programs often include no-email days, tech-free meetings, and digital detox retreats.

2. **Personal Success Stories**: Many individuals who have undertaken digital detoxes report feeling more balanced, present,

and less stressed. They often experience improved sleep, better relationships, and enhanced creativity.

3. **Educational Settings**: Schools and universities that encourage digital detox periods, especially during exams, have noted better academic performance and reduced anxiety among students.

Overcoming Challenges in Digital Detox

While the benefits of a digital detox are clear, there can be challenges in implementing it:

1. **Withdrawal Symptoms**: Initially, some individuals may experience anxiety or restlessness when disconnecting from their devices. It's important to push through this phase and focus on the benefits.

2. **Social Pressure**: The expectation to be constantly available can make it difficult to take a digital break. Communicating your plans and setting boundaries can help manage this pressure.

3. **Work Requirements**: For many, work necessitates constant connectivity. Finding a balance and setting specific times to unplug, even if briefly, can still be beneficial.

4. **Habits and Addiction**: Breaking the habit of reaching for digital devices requires conscious effort and discipline. Gradual reduction in screen time rather than abrupt cessation can be a more manageable approach.

Conclusion

In a world increasingly dominated by digital interactions, the need for a digital detox is more important than ever. Taking regular breaks from technology can significantly enhance mental, emotional, and physical well-being. By understanding the impact of constant connectivity and adopting practical strategies for digital detox, individuals can achieve a healthier balance and enjoy the benefits of both the digital and physical worlds.

In the next chapter, we will explore the ethical considerations surrounding data privacy in the digital age, examining how personal data is collected, used, and protected in an increasingly interconnected world. Through this exploration, we aim to provide insights into maintaining privacy and security while engaging with digital technologies.

CHAPTER 11: THE ROLE OF TECHNOLOGY IN EDUCATION AND LEARNING

Introduction

The integration of technology in education has transformed traditional teaching and learning methods. From primary schools to universities, technological advancements have revolutionised how educators teach and students learn. This chapter explores the multifaceted role of technology in education, its benefits and challenges, and how it shapes the future of learning.

Historical Context

To understand the current landscape, it is essential to consider the evolution of technology in education. Initially, educational technology included simple tools such as blackboards and overhead projectors. The advent of computers in the 1980s and the internet in the 1990s marked significant milestones, enabling more interactive and resource-rich educational experiences. Today, digital platforms, artificial intelligence, and virtual reality are pushing the boundaries of what is possible in education.

Technological Tools and Innovations

1. **Digital Classrooms**: Virtual learning environments (VLEs) such as Moodle and Blackboard facilitate online courses, enabling students to access lectures, assignments, and resources anytime and anywhere. These platforms support blended learning, combining online and face-to-face education.

2. **Interactive Whiteboards**: These tools replace traditional blackboards, allowing teachers to present multimedia content interactively. They engage students through visuals, animations, and real-time problem-solving activities.

3. **Educational Apps and Software**: A plethora of apps and software tools support various aspects of learning, from language acquisition (Duolingo) to mathematics (Khan Academy) and beyond. These resources personalise learning, catering to individual student needs and pacing.

4. **E-books and Online Libraries**: Digital books and online libraries offer vast resources that are easily accessible. Platforms like Google Books and Project Gutenberg provide access to a wide range of texts, supporting research and learning.

5. **Virtual Reality (VR) and Augmented Reality (AR)**: VR and AR technologies create immersive learning experiences. For example, students can take virtual field trips to historical sites or explore the human body in 3D, enhancing their understanding through experiential learning.

6. **Artificial Intelligence (AI)**: AI-powered tools such as intelligent tutoring systems (ITS) and chatbots provide personalised learning experiences and instant feedback, helping students to progress at their own pace and offering support when needed.

Benefits of Technology in Education

1. **Personalised Learning**: Technology enables personalised learning paths, allowing students to learn at their own pace and style. Adaptive learning systems assess individual progress and tailor content to meet specific needs.

2. **Enhanced Engagement**: Interactive tools and multimedia content make learning more engaging and enjoyable. Gamification, which incorporates game elements into learning, motivates students and enhances their involvement.

3. **Accessibility and Inclusion**: Technology breaks down barriers to education, providing access to learners regardless of geographical location or physical disabilities. Tools such as screen readers and speech-to-text software support inclusive learning environments.

4. **Collaboration and Communication**: Online platforms facilitate collaboration among students and teachers. Tools like Google Classroom and Microsoft Teams enable real-time communication, group work, and resource sharing.

5. **Resource Availability**: The internet provides access to an unprecedented amount of information and resources, supporting research and expanding learning opportunities beyond traditional textbooks.

6. **Efficiency and Organisation**: Digital tools streamline administrative tasks, such as grading and attendance, allowing educators to focus more on teaching. Organisational tools help students manage their time and coursework effectively.

Challenges of Technology in Education

1. **Digital Divide**: Access to technology is not uniform across different regions and socio-economic groups. The digital divide can exacerbate educational inequalities, leaving some students behind.

2. **Screen Time and Health**: Excessive screen time can lead to health issues such as eye strain, poor posture, and decreased

physical activity. Balancing screen time with offline activities is essential for student well-being.

3. **Cybersecurity and Privacy**: The use of digital tools raises concerns about data privacy and cybersecurity. Protecting student information and ensuring secure online interactions are critical.

4. **Dependency on Technology**: Over-reliance on technology can reduce critical thinking and problem-solving skills. It is important to integrate technology in a way that complements rather than replaces traditional learning methods.

5. **Teacher Training and Support**: Effective integration of technology requires adequate training and support for educators. Ongoing professional development is necessary to keep up with technological advancements and implement them effectively.

Case Studies and Success Stories

1. **Flipped Classrooms**: The flipped classroom model, where students watch lectures at home and engage in interactive activities in class, has shown success in enhancing understanding and retention. Schools implementing this model report higher student engagement and improved academic performance.

2. **One-to-One Programs**: Initiatives like One Laptop per Child (OLPC) provide each student with a personal device, aiming to improve educational outcomes. Studies have shown that these programs increase digital literacy and provide more personalised learning experiences.

3. **MOOCs (Massive Open Online Courses) **: Platforms like Coursera and edX offer free or affordable courses from top universities to a global audience. MOOCs have democratized education, providing access to high-quality learning resources to anyone with an internet connection.

4. **AI Tutoring Systems**: AI tutoring systems like Carnegie Learning have demonstrated significant improvements in student performance, particularly in subjects like mathematics. These

systems provide personalised support and instant feedback, helping students grasp complex concepts.

Future Trends in Educational Technology

1. **Artificial Intelligence and Machine Learning**: AI and machine learning will continue to enhance personalised learning, predictive analytics, and intelligent content delivery.

2. **Virtual and Augmented Reality**: VR and AR technologies will become more widespread, providing immersive and interactive learning experiences in various subjects.

3. **Blockchain Technology**: Blockchain can revolutionise educational credentials, ensuring secure and verifiable records of academic achievements and certifications.

4. **Gamification and Game-Based Learning**: The use of game elements in education will increase, making learning more engaging and motivating for students.

5. **Data Analytics**: Advanced data analytics will provide deeper insights into student performance, enabling more effective interventions and support.

Conclusion

Technology has undeniably reshaped the educational landscape, offering numerous benefits and presenting new challenges. As we move forward, it is crucial to harness the potential of technology to enhance learning while addressing its drawbacks. By promoting digital literacy, ensuring equitable access, and maintaining a balanced approach, we can create a future where technology and education work hand in hand to foster growth and development.

In the next chapter, we will delve into the ethical considerations of data privacy in the digital age. We will explore how personal data is collected, used, and protected, and discuss the implications for individuals and society.

CHAPTER 12: THE FUTURE OF WORK: REMOTE WORKING AND DIGITAL COLLABORATION

Introduction

The future of work is undergoing a transformative shift, largely driven by advancements in technology and changing societal norms. Remote working and digital collaboration, once considered niche or temporary solutions, have become central to modern work environments. This chapter explores the evolution of remote work, the tools that facilitate digital collaboration, the benefits and challenges of these practices, and the implications for the future of work.

Evolution of Remote Working

Remote working, also known as telecommuting, has evolved significantly over the past few decades. Initially, it was a privilege limited to certain professions and senior-level employees. However, with the advent of high-speed internet, cloud computing, and sophisticated collaboration tools, remote work has become more accessible and widespread.

1. **Early Beginnings**: In the 1970s and 1980s, remote working was primarily associated with freelancers, consultants, and telemarketers. The concept gained traction as technology improved and companies sought ways to reduce office overheads.

2. **Technological Advancements**: The rise of the internet in the 1990s and early 2000s enabled more robust communication and data sharing. Email, instant messaging, and early collaboration platforms like Skype began to facilitate remote work.

3. **Mainstream Adoption**: The 2010s saw a significant increase in remote working as cloud-based tools, project management software, and video conferencing technologies matured. Companies like Google, Microsoft, and Slack developed platforms that made remote work seamless and efficient.

4. **Pandemic Accelerated Shift**: The COVID-19 pandemic in 2020 forced a rapid and widespread adoption of remote work. Many organisations, having experienced the viability and benefits of remote work during the crisis, have continued to support it even post-pandemic.

Digital Collaboration Tools

Effective remote working relies heavily on digital collaboration tools that enable communication, project management, and team collaboration. Key tools include:

1. **Video Conferencing**: Platforms like Zoom, Microsoft Teams, and Google Meet facilitate virtual meetings, webinars, and face-to-face interactions despite geographical distances.

2. **Instant Messaging**: Tools such as Slack, Microsoft Teams, and WhatsApp provide real-time communication, fostering quick interactions and team discussions.

3. **Project Management**: Software like Trello, Asana, and Jira help teams track projects, assign tasks, and monitor progress, ensuring that work stays on track and deadlines are met.

4. **Cloud Storage and File Sharing**: Services like Google Drive, Dropbox, and OneDrive allow teams to store, share, and collaborate on documents and files securely and efficiently.

5. **Collaboration Platforms**: Integrated platforms like Microsoft 365 and Google Workspace offer a suite of tools for communication, document creation, and project management, enabling a cohesive work environment.

Benefits of Remote Working and Digital Collaboration

1. **Flexibility and Work-Life Balance**: Remote work offers employees the flexibility to design their work schedules around personal commitments, leading to improved work-life balance and job satisfaction.

2. **Increased Productivity**: Many studies have shown that remote workers are often more productive due to fewer office distractions, reduced commuting time, and the ability to work in a preferred environment.

3. **Cost Savings**: Both employers and employees can save on costs related to commuting, office space, and other overheads. Companies can reduce their physical office footprint and associated expenses.

4. **Access to a Global Talent Pool**: Remote work allows companies to hire talent from anywhere in the world, overcoming geographical limitations and benefiting from diverse skills and perspectives.

5. **Environmental Impact**: Reduced commuting and less need for large office spaces contribute to lower carbon emissions and a smaller environmental footprint.

Challenges of Remote Working and Digital Collaboration

1. **Communication Barriers**: Lack of face-to-face interactions can lead to misunderstandings, miscommunication, and feelings of isolation among team members.

2. **Technological Dependence**: Remote work relies heavily on technology, and any disruptions (e.g., internet outages, software glitches) can significantly impact productivity.

3. **Security Concerns**: Ensuring data security and protecting sensitive information can be more challenging in a remote work setup. Companies need robust cybersecurity measures to mitigate risks.

4. **Work-Life Boundaries**: The blurring of work and personal life boundaries can lead to overworking and burnout. It is crucial to establish clear boundaries and practices to maintain a healthy work-life balance.

5. **Team Cohesion and Culture**: Building and maintaining a strong organisational culture and team cohesion can be difficult without regular in-person interactions. Companies need to find creative ways to foster team spirit and a sense of belonging.

Strategies for Effective Remote Working and Digital Collaboration

1. **Clear Communication**: Establishing clear communication channels and protocols is essential. Regular check-ins, virtual meetings, and transparent sharing of information help keep everyone aligned.

2. **Effective Use of Tools**: Choosing the right digital collaboration tools and ensuring that all team members are trained to use them effectively is crucial for seamless collaboration.

3. **Regular Team Building**: Virtual team-building activities, online social events, and periodic in-person meetings can help strengthen team bonds and maintain a positive work culture.

4. **Flexible Work Policies**: Implementing flexible work policies that allow for different working styles and schedules can help accommodate individual needs and preferences.

5. **Focus on Well-being**: Encouraging employees to take breaks, set boundaries, and prioritise their well-being is important to prevent burnout and maintain productivity.

The Future of Work

The future of work is likely to be a hybrid model, combining the benefits of remote work with the advantages of in-person interactions. Key trends include:

1. **Hybrid Work Environments**: Many companies are adopting hybrid models, where employees can choose to work remotely or from the office based on their needs and preferences.

2. **Increased Focus on Employee Experience**: Organisations will place greater emphasis on creating positive employee experiences, supporting well-being, and fostering a sense of community, regardless of work location.

3. **Technological Innovations**: Continued advancements in AI, virtual reality, and collaboration tools will further enhance remote work capabilities and experiences.

4. **Redesigning Workspaces**: Physical office spaces will be redesigned to support flexible working, with a focus on collaborative areas, hot-desking, and technology integration.

5. **Policy and Regulation**: Governments and organisations will need to adapt policies and regulations to support remote work, addressing issues such as taxation, labour laws, and data privacy.

Conclusion

Remote working and digital collaboration have fundamentally reshaped the way we work, offering numerous benefits and presenting new challenges. As we navigate the future of work, it is crucial to leverage technology effectively, foster a positive work culture, and prioritise employee well-being. By embracing the opportunities and addressing the challenges, we can create a more flexible, inclusive, and productive work environment.

In the next chapter, we will delve into the ethical considerations surrounding data privacy in the digital age. We will explore how personal data is collected, used, and protected, and discuss the implications for individuals and society.

CHAPTER 13: PRIVACY AND SECURITY IN THE AGE OF SOCIAL MEDIA

Introduction

In today's digital world, social media has become an integral part of our lives, offering unprecedented connectivity and information sharing. However, this convenience comes with significant concerns regarding privacy and security. This chapter delves into the complex landscape of privacy and security in the age of social media, examining the risks, challenges, and measures individuals and organisations can take to protect themselves.

The Evolution of Privacy Concerns

The concept of privacy has evolved dramatically with the advent of social media. Traditional notions of privacy, which primarily revolved around physical spaces and personal information, have been fundamentally altered in the digital age. Key factors contributing to this evolution include:

1. **Data Explosion**: Social media platforms encourage users to share vast amounts of personal data, including photos, location, and daily activities, often without fully understanding the implications.

2. **Surveillance and Data Collection**: Companies collect extensive data on user behaviour for targeted advertising, creating detailed profiles that can be exploited or misused.

3. **Lack of Awareness**: Many users are unaware of the extent to which their data is collected and used, leading to a false sense of security.

Risks Associated with Social Media

The widespread use of social media presents several privacy and security risks, including:

1. **Data Breaches**: Social media platforms are frequent targets of cyberattacks, leading to massive data breaches that expose personal information.

2. **Identity Theft**: Personal information shared on social media can be used by malicious actors to steal identities and commit fraud.

3. **Phishing Attacks**: Cybercriminals use social media to launch phishing attacks, tricking users into revealing sensitive information or clicking on malicious links.

4. **Social Engineering**: Hackers exploit information shared on social media to manipulate individuals into divulging confidential information or performing actions that compromise security.

5. **Cyberbullying and Harassment**: The anonymity provided by social media can lead to cyberbullying, harassment,

and other forms of online abuse, impacting mental health and well-being.

Protecting Privacy on Social Media

To safeguard privacy on social media, users should adopt proactive measures and best practices. Key strategies include:

1. **Privacy Settings**: Regularly review and update privacy settings on social media platforms to control who can see your information and posts.

2. **Limit Sharing**: Be mindful of the personal information you share online. Avoid posting sensitive details such as home addresses, phone numbers, or financial information.

3. **Strong Passwords and Two-Factor Authentication**: Use strong, unique passwords for each social media account and enable two-factor authentication to add an extra layer of security.

4. **Be Wary of Links and Requests**: Exercise caution when clicking on links or accepting friend requests from unknown individuals, as they may be phishing attempts or malicious actors.

5. **Regular Audits**: Periodically audit your social media presence to identify and remove any outdated or unnecessary personal information.

Organisational Responsibilities and Best Practices

Organisations also play a crucial role in protecting user privacy and ensuring security on social media platforms. Key responsibilities and best practices include:

1. **Data Protection Policies**: Implement robust data protection policies that comply with relevant regulations such as the General Data Protection Regulation (GDPR) or the California Consumer Privacy Act (CCPA).

2. **Security Measures**: Invest in advanced security measures, including encryption, intrusion detection systems, and regular security audits, to protect user data from breaches.

3. **Transparency**: Be transparent with users about data collection practices and how their information is used. Provide clear, accessible privacy policies and consent forms.

4. **User Education**: Educate users about privacy risks and best practices through awareness campaigns, tutorials, and resources.

5. **Incident Response Plans**: Develop and maintain incident response plans to quickly and effectively address data breaches and other security incidents.

Legal and Regulatory Landscape

The legal and regulatory landscape surrounding privacy and security on social media is continually evolving. Key developments include:

1. **General Data Protection Regulation (GDPR)**: Implemented in the European Union in 2018, the GDPR sets stringent requirements for data protection and privacy, significantly impacting how companies handle user data.

2. **California Consumer Privacy Act (CCPA)**: Enacted in 2020, the CCPA grants California residents greater control over their personal information and imposes strict data protection requirements on businesses.

3. **Privacy Shield**: The EU-US Privacy Shield framework, although invalidated in 2020, highlighted the importance of cross-border data transfer regulations and the need for robust privacy protections.

4. **Emerging Legislation**: Countries around the world are enacting or updating privacy laws to address the challenges posed by social media and digital data. This includes laws focused on data localisation, user consent, and data breach notification.

Future Trends and Considerations

As social media continues to evolve, so too will the challenges and opportunities related to privacy and security. Key trends and considerations for the future include:

1. **Artificial Intelligence and Privacy**: AI-powered tools can enhance security by detecting and mitigating threats, but they also raise concerns about data privacy and surveillance.

2. **Decentralised Social Networks**: Emerging decentralised social networks aim to give users more control over their data and reduce reliance on centralised platforms that collect and monetise personal information.

3. **Enhanced Encryption**: Advances in encryption technologies will play a critical role in protecting user data from cyber threats and ensuring privacy.

4. **User Empowerment**: Greater emphasis on user empowerment and data sovereignty will drive the development of tools and platforms that prioritise user privacy and consent.

5. **Ethical Considerations**: The ethical implications of data collection and surveillance will continue to be a focal point of discussion, influencing policy, regulation, and corporate practices.

Conclusion

Privacy and security in the age of social media are complex and multifaceted issues that require ongoing attention and adaptation. By understanding the risks, adopting best practices, and staying informed about regulatory developments, individuals and organisations can better navigate the digital landscape and protect their privacy. As technology evolves, so too must our approaches to privacy and security, ensuring that social media remains a safe and empowering space for all users.

In the next chapter, we will explore the psychological impact of social media on self-esteem and body image, examining how online interactions and content can influence our perceptions of ourselves and others.

CONCLUSION: NAVIGATING THE DIGITAL WORLD

Introduction

The digital age, characterized by rapid technological advancements and the omnipresence of social media, has significantly altered the way we live, work, and interact with one another. As we navigate this complex landscape, it is essential to understand the multifaceted impacts of enhanced technology and social sites on our psychology, relationships, and society at large. This conclusion synthesizes the key insights from our exploration and offers guidance for effectively managing our digital lives.

The Psychological Shift

The integration of technology into our daily routines has brought about profound psychological shifts. Social media platforms, while offering unprecedented connectivity and access to information, also present challenges related to mental health, self-esteem, and social comparison. The constant exposure to curated and often idealized portrayals of life can lead to feelings of inadequacy and anxiety. Recognizing these effects is the first step toward mitigating their impact.

Enhanced Connectivity and Social Interaction

Social media has revolutionized the way we interact, creating new forms of communication and community building. Online relationships, whether friendships or romantic connections, offer opportunities for meaningful engagement but also require careful navigation to avoid pitfalls such as cyberbullying, misinformation, and the erosion of offline social skills. Balancing online and offline interactions is crucial for maintaining healthy social connections.

The Role of Algorithms

Algorithms play a pivotal role in shaping our online experiences, influencing the content we see and the interactions we have. While they can enhance user experience by personalizing content, they also raise concerns about echo chambers, misinformation, and manipulation. Understanding how algorithms work and being critical of the content they deliver can help users make more informed choices about their online consumption.

Cyberpsychology and Online Behaviour

Cyberpsychology, the study of how technology affects human behaviour, provides valuable insights into our online actions and reactions. It highlights the importance of self-awareness and digital literacy in navigating the digital world. By understanding the psychological principles at play, individuals can better manage their online presence and interactions.

Technology and Mental Health

The impact of technology on mental health is a double-edged sword. While digital tools and platforms can offer support and resources for mental well-being, they can also contribute to stress, anxiety, and depression. Strategies such as digital detoxing, setting boundaries, and using technology mindfully are essential for maintaining mental health in the digital age.

Crafting Digital Identities

In the digital world, identity construction is a dynamic and ongoing process. Users craft their personas online through social media profiles, posts, and interactions. While this offers opportunities for self-expression and connection, it also requires a careful balance to ensure authenticity and protect personal privacy. Being mindful of the digital footprint we leave behind is crucial.

The Influence of Social Media on Self-Esteem and Body Image

Social media's impact on self-esteem and body image is significant, particularly among younger users. Exposure to idealized images and lifestyles can lead to negative self-perception and body dissatisfaction. Promoting diverse and realistic representations and fostering a critical approach to online content are essential steps in mitigating these effects.

The Social Comparison Theory in the Digital Age

Social comparison, a natural human tendency, is amplified in the digital age. The constant comparison with peers and influencers on social media can affect self-esteem and well-being. Recognizing the pitfalls of social comparison and cultivating a healthy self-concept can help individuals navigate these challenges.

Online Relationships: Friendship, Romance, and Community

Online platforms offer new avenues for forming and maintaining relationships. While these relationships can be meaningful and supportive, they also require attention to authenticity, communication, and boundaries. Building trust and understanding in online interactions is key to fostering healthy digital relationships.

Digital Detox: The Need for a Break from Technology

Taking breaks from technology, or digital detoxing, is increasingly recognized as essential for mental and emotional well-being. Periodic disconnection allows individuals to recharge, reflect, and reconnect with the offline world. Establishing regular digital detox practices can help mitigate the negative effects of constant connectivity.

The Role of Technology in Education and Learning

Technology has transformed education and learning, offering new tools and platforms for knowledge acquisition and skill development. While it enhances access and flexibility, it also requires critical evaluation to ensure the quality and efficacy of digital learning experiences. Integrating technology thoughtfully into educational practices can maximize its benefits.

The Future of Work: Remote Working and Digital Collaboration

The future of work is increasingly digital, with remote working and digital collaboration becoming the norm. These changes offer flexibility and access to global talent but also present challenges related to communication, security, and work-life balance. Adapting to these changes involves leveraging technology effectively while maintaining a focus on well-being and productivity.

Privacy and Security in the Age of Social Media

Privacy and security are paramount concerns in the digital age. Protecting personal information and navigating the risks associated with social media require awareness and proactive measures. Understanding the regulatory landscape, adopting best practices, and staying informed about emerging threats are essential for safeguarding privacy and security.

Conclusion: Embracing a Balanced Digital Life

As we continue to integrate technology into our lives, it is essential to strike a balance that maximizes the benefits while mitigating the risks. This involves being mindful of our digital consumption, prioritizing mental and emotional well-being, and fostering healthy relationships both online and offline. By staying informed, critical, and proactive, we can navigate the digital world with confidence and resilience.

The journey through the digital landscape is ongoing and ever-evolving. Embracing continuous learning, adaptability, and a balanced approach will enable us to thrive in this dynamic environment. The key is to harness the power of technology for positive growth while being vigilant about its potential pitfalls. As we move forward, let us strive to create a digital world that enhances our lives, supports our well-being, and fosters genuine connection and understanding.

www.ingramcontent.com/pod-product-compliance
Lightning Source LLC
Chambersburg PA
CBHW071956210526
45479CB00003B/960